MEASURING
OURSELVES

Measuring

OURSELVES

TAKING MEASURABLE STEPS TO CAREER ADVANCEMENT

Michael W. Hill

Contents

This book is dedicated to those employees who realize: "If I'm going to get ahead, it's up to me."

INTRODUCTION

Ever wonder why some people you know are always getting the promotion? Why some people are always getting the raise that is higher than everyone else's?

Do you also wonder why some people sit back and have very little motivation to get anything more out of life than what falls in their lap?

The difference is that the first group has made a conscious decision to evaluate their professional career on an ongoing basis. They are individuals who have set goals for themselves and then systematically gauge their progress toward accomplishing those goals.

This book will teach you five traits that will help you challenge yourself to become happier-and more successful in your business career.

This book will teach you that by measuring yourself and acting on those measurements you can accomplish any professional goal you set.

This book will show you that average is not good enough. "Good enough" never is.

This book will help you set "full potential" goals for yourself so that when you finish a project you know it truly is your personal best. The kind of work that gets recognized as superior, the kind that earns the financial recognition you want.

This book will teach you to: set challenging goals, break those goals down into measurable accomplishments, and measure-evaluate-proceed on the goals. In addition, it will teach you how to keep yourself motivated.

This book will teach you that with ordinary ability and extraordinary perseverance anything is attainable. Don't let intellect intimidate you. As Malcolm Gladwell states, "intellect and achievement are far from perfectly correlated."

One definition of success is...to be able to spend your life in your own way. ***Measuring Ourselves*** will introduce techniques you will be able to use to lay out a personal plan for achieving your desired level of success.

We've all heard the phrase, "If you continue to do what you've always done, you will continue to get what you've always gotten." Through ***Measuring Ourselves*** techniques, you will change what you've always been doing to get the results you've always desired.

CHAPTER

1

Why We Don't Reach Our Full Potential

Change your thoughts and you change your world.

Norman Vincent Peale

Author, Professional Speaker

Why We Don't Reach Our Full Potential

People don't reach their full potential for a variety of reasons: they are too overwhelmed, not smart enough, too shy, too tall, or too lazy. In our business careers the excuses are just as exaggerated: I didn't go to the correct school, I never received my MBA, or I didn't inherit a family business.

All of us can dream up as many excuses as we want. The truth of the matter is that everyone has a lot of excuses available to them. In this book you will be presented with a system to overcome any legitimate reasons for not reaching your full potential and you will become a person who looks past any excuses.

Let's explore some of the reasons people give for not reaching their full potential. One reason is lack of preparation. You've heard: "Never wait until you need something before you act." However, we have all done this. We sign up to run a half-marathon with our friends, we fail to train sufficiently and then we're disappointed in our finishing time... or worse, we fail to finish. In business it happens all the time — the raise or promotion goes to the employee who has done that little bit extra, the one who is constantly learning...reading about new trends and ideas in industry magazines, the one who purchases that recent business bestseller and actually learns a new process or procedure, not the one who spends the same time on hobbies or studying baseball, poker or Nascar statistics.

A good friend of mine just got a wonderful promotion because in addition to doing his job he took a class at the local community college, thus becoming educated in an area the company needed expertise in.

Always bear in mind that your own
resolution to succeed is more important than any other one thing.

Abraham Lincoln
16th President of the United States

We need to discover exactly what we want, turn that "want" into a goal, and make specific plans or define smaller steps to lead us to accomplishing our desired outcomes.

Another reason we don't reach our full potential is fear: fear of failure, fear of missing our targets, fear of not living up to others' expectations. Fear afflicts individuals as well as groups of individuals (companies). Fear is contagious.

This book will show you how to break down any fear to overcome it with measurable accomplishments. This book will also show you that when you become accomplished in goal setting, it's not others' expectations you live up to. It's your own.

It is important to remember that you yourself are ultimately responsible for your own success.

Susan A. DePhillips
Corporate Confidential

Why don't we reach our full potential? It takes discipline. Discipline can make the difference between merely adequate and really first-rate work. When we are handed a setback we pick one of two options. We either withdraw and wait for hard times to pass or we become aggressive and investigate what has gone wrong, adjust and move forward. Most people assume the former, rather than latter, position.

Most of us know what it takes to succeed, we just lack the discipline to make it happen. Truly successful people have found the time and energy to step back, evaluate their goals and make plans to achieve them. In sports it takes training and practice; in business it takes a different type of training: education!

Like in the previous example. Was it easy to attend a class two nights a week? No. Was it easy to set time aside during the week to study and do assignments? No. However, was there a nice reward for him at the conclusion? Yes!

Discipline allows us to make plans, execute those plans, and adjust when an outcome is presented to us that we didn't expect. Discipline instills confidence. We've all been told, "Don't put on an act"; however by acting confident we then feel confident, leading to accomplishments.

We've all seen examples of confidence, like the professional speaker who displays so much confidence giving his presentation he receives a standing ovation at the end. We've also all seen people lacking confidence who believe by "winging it" they'll get by.

Expect more to get more. Good leaders constantly stretch people. Successful individuals constantly stretch themselves.

Michael W. Hill

People often take the hard road rather than the easy road. There's an easy and a hard way to learn anything. The hard way is by trial and error. The easy way is by learning from others. Many people enter into a business environment thinking it will take an unknown number of years to learn the industry. In hindsight they find out that a weekend seminar or appropriate business book could bring them up to speed very quickly.

Life is too short and there are countless things to experience and achieve. Use trial and error as your last means of education, not your first.

Why don't we reach our full potential? We don't get ourselves prepared enough for when that "one" opportunity presents itself. Let's take a look at the business world. Who gets the promotion? It's not the employee who has done the same thing for the last year-or even 10 years. The promotion goes to the individual who has taken the extra effort to become educated in different areas of the business.

Most companies offer some type of tuition re-imbursement, but I'm constantly amazed at the number of employees who don't take advantage of it.

No one except yourself has a vested
interest in your success.

Susan A. DePhillips
Author

Another reason we don't reach our full potential: We don't want to take ownership and responsibility for who we are. Taking responsibility for your work eliminates the possible excuses for why we're not performing at a top level.

Average performers are looking for the most comfortable position they can find. How many times have you heard someone say, "As soon as my 401(k) is up to a certain amount, I'm set"? Some people even make the statement, "As soon as I have my house paid off, I'll be sitting pretty." These generally are the same people who would rather make an additional contribution to their 401(k) or additional house payment than take that money and invest in themselves and become a more productive, higher-paid person. These are also the individuals who can't wait until the weekend or their next vacation. You know them, the ones who make those big Xs or slash marks on their calendar when the day is done. This book will show you how to make that X on your calendar at the end of the day, right before you go to bed, because you did the best you could toward a set goal established for that day.

Mountain climbers are fond of saying, "It's not the mountain we conquer, but ourselves." It takes a lot of determination to break out of our self-imposed molds and "conquer" ourselves.

Imagine how hard it is for someone to work in the business world for 20 years, 8 to 5, every day, drive home to chilled wine, grilled burgers on the deck and a new CD playing in the background. Now imagine that same person earning an MBA. While still working 8 to 5, drives home, has a quick dinner, no wine—needs to read/study, gets on-line, writes a paper. Passes the course, and then signs up for the *next* course.

I would propose that the effort to conquer either quest — a mountain summit or earning an advanced degree — takes the same amount of self-discipline and courage.

The most amazing thing about becoming someone who accomplishes goals is the momentum it sets in place to accomplish more goals.

Why don't we realize our full potential? We want to wait for just the right moment. If we wait for the moment when everything, absolutely everything, is ready, we will never begin. How many of us set January 1 as the date to do the following: stop smoking or drinking, or start going to church or the gym? Research has found that you're likely to stick with a self-imposed program no matter when you start. Why wait?

Why don't we realize our full potential? Costs! John F. Kennedy is quoted to have said, "There are costs and risks to a program of action, but they are far less than the long-range risks and costs of comfortable inaction." President Kennedy was referring to different actions he needed to take at the time to make the United States and ultimately the world a safer place. However, his statement can be applied to individuals. What is the cost of putting together a program to reach your full potential?

Let's use exercise as an example. What are the costs of beginning an exercise program? Possible costs include joining a fitness center or the cost of buying exercise equipment for your home. You can also start a very nice program using your floor and doing push-ups and sit-ups with no monetary outlay. I'm partial to jumping rope: investment $1.99. (I bet you can't jump for five minutes.) What's the cost of comfortable inaction?

Why don't we realize our full potential? It takes incredibly hard work, persistence, and sacrifice, three traits most of us only have for those things we're passionate about. To reach full potential we must apply these traits to all areas of our lives, professional and personal.

I'm sure at one time or another you have been congratulated for a job well done when you knew you could have done better. Through the system of setting goals for yourself, and tracking your progress toward those goals, you will experience the feeling of self-satisfaction-knowing you just finished your best work.

Often what prevents us from reaching our full potential is lack of energy. This can be either physical or mental energy. The most successful individuals are those who know how to build an energy reserve and call on it when needed. This book will teach you how to call on that reserve.

You might just throw up your hands and say, "Well, these are the cards I was dealt, so what can I do?" The individuals living up to their full potential take a look at their dealt hand and learn to play it into the winning hand.

There are individuals all around us who have risen to a challenge that most of us thought would be insurmountable. Just read the daily paper and you'll see examples in every section.

- Lance Armstrong overcomes testicular cancer to win the Tour de France seven times.
- Nelson Mandela is sentenced to prison for life. He keeps a positive spirit, never lets go of his personal beliefs, is finally set free and becomes a leader of his country.
- Bruce Springsteen in his early days has a legal dispute with a producer and is basically banned from the music scene. Through personal perseverance he later goes on to become one of the top performers of his generation.

I've recently worked with a group of businessmen in Indianapolis who started a business selling a product. For the first two years sales did not go well. So, they changed to selling the "service" for the product and that business has taken off for them.

How many of us would have chosen a different path than any of the above-mentioned men, if one of those roadblocks had been put in front of us?

Each man had his goals, he had a plan and he decided early-on how he was going to measure himself as he attempted to reach his ultimate goal.

The human race is strange. We know most things we want take hard work, but we are always looking, searching for the easy way out. I think it's partially caused by the fact that occasionally we do find a quick fix.

If we truly evaluate the situation, however, we will find the reason something seemed like a quick fix was because we were more ready than we thought when the right opportunity presented itself.

Through careful goal setting and measurement, we can prepare ourselves for that **moment of opportunity** that eventually presents itself to all of us.

Every day we are on the stage performing, whether it is on a court or in a company. We need to evaluate and analyze our performance. Did I truly do my best, and if not, what do I need to do to improve?

What we need to do is analyze both good performances and poor. There are lessons to be learned from both. Why were we able to perform in such a way one time and not the next?

Consultant Michael Staver recommends individuals accept their current circumstances and take responsibility. "Acceptance" of a less-than-ideal situation is step one; the next step is to respond to the situation. It's all about response; do something-anything-to start you toward your desired outcome.

Why are Olympic athletes performing at such a high level nowadays? It's mainly because of the evaluation they go through constantly: muscle mass, lean index versus body fat, lung capacity, different weight-lifting performance numbers, and oxygen consumption rate, to name just a few.

Just think of what's available currently for business people. In addition to good old-fashioned books from the library, there's a bookstore in every strip-mall or books on tape, CDs, and now the "Kindel." There are live seminars, taped seminars, web-cast seminars. There are a lot of ways to elevate your performance.

Look at an example from your own career. Look at the last successful presentation you gave to a group at work. Why was it a hit? More research into the topic? More expert opinions, more charts, more graphs?

Most of our work is never truly evaluated or measured by others. Don't let this stop you from evaluating yourself. Write it down, just like you would want your boss to do. If it's as good as you think, present your own evaluation to the boss at the appropriate time!

There's only one true evaluation of us, and that is an evaluation *of ourselves, by ourselves.* We are the ones who know if we truly preformed to the level we know we are capable of.

Athletes are very good at self-evaluation. We should learn from them. How many times have we heard the winning golfer on Sunday afternoon proclaim, "I could have had a score two strokes lower if I hadn't missed those easy putts on 2 and 16"? Within minutes of the end of their performance they've announced to the viewing public where they could have done better and oftentimes they go on to tell why. I pulled the putt, I pushed the putt, I lost my concentration thinking of the easy hole coming up next.

What a way for us to make ourselves better businesspeople! At the end of the day or even midday, measure yourself. Such questions as: how am I doing toward accomplishing today's goals? What have I done correctly? What have I done poorly? What can I learn to make tomorrow better?

Life has a tendency to put a lot of obstacles in our everyday paths. For many of us, it's a full-time job taking care of these. We sure don't need to put any additional, self-imposed problems in our way. Sometimes our roadblocks are internal, sometimes they are external forces. Both can be either devastating or rejuvenating when we're trying to accomplish our goals.

Almost anything in excess can lead to additional problems we will need to deal with. Evaluate and measure your life to see if it's in balance. Too much eating, drinking, or smoking, to name a few negative/destructive behaviors, will hinder our performance.

Let's look at excessive eating, the cause of obesity. It's been estimated that 60-70 percent of the population is obese. This is a very limiting factor in achieving your full potential. How you feel determines how well you do. If you're overweight your energy level suffers and thus your performance.

Just as others' performance influences our performance, our performance and examples can influence others. There's probably no greater influence than a parent with his or her child. The parent who allows the child to do just enough to slide by is not setting a good example for a future top performer.

Other bad influences are all around us. The spouse who suggests calling in sick the day of an important meeting... or how many "gimmee" putts have you taken that probably shouldn't have been? All of these forces, whether good or bad, have a way of building up and influencing your future behavior. *Learn from the bad forces and mimic the good.*

People working to their full potential with measurable goals know how to shut themselves down on one project and focus on another. A person reaching full potential is not a workaholic in any one area, but rather a well-rounded person achieving goals—physically, mentally, and spiritually. Others won't be making fun of you and asking *why*; they'll be wanting to meet with you to discuss *how* you do what you do.

Imitation is the best form of flattery. Individuals who are reaching their full potential in an area, or those who have already reached it, are imitated all the time. How many successful businessmen have written books and then, as if overnight, all businesses are mimicking their techniques?

You can either take action or you can
hang back and hope for a miracle.
Peter F. Drucker
Author, Management Consultant

In the following chapters in **Measuring Ourselves** you will be given the knowledge for how, when and why to take action.

Measuring our performance is an ongoing process which, when mastered, will enable us to take control of our own destiny. Any peak performer will tell you the act of making the commitment is the *how.* Is it a tough decision? Definitely! But peak performers say that once the large decision is clearly made, nine times out of ten you can make the rest fall in place easily.

The main reason we don't reach our full potential is that we don't set goals, or we don't set our goals high enough. We settle for the status quo or in most cases less than average.

Feedback is the key to improving any performance. Most people never receive feedback from others. Without this feedback it's hard to succeed, so we must find ways to measure ourselves.

In business, good evaluations are done sparingly, if at all. Some evaluations, even for top managers, are only given through the process of checking the appropriate boxes, which the supervisor hopes will not offend the employee.

In sports our coaches compliment the best performers and berate the poor performers, but the majority of the team, those in the middle, get no feedback at all.

We need to measure ourselves because in most cases no one else is going to! Subsequent chapters will teach you how to be your own coach, cheerleader, and trainer, to accomplish those things you truly desire.

Nothing great was ever achieved without enthusiasm. We need to find ways to get ourselves excited about life. Normally if we take the time to focus on our goals-really focus — enthusiasm will develop. Picture yourself in the corner office, on your new boat, or at a summit of the Grand Tetons. Focusing and forming the mental picture of accomplishment will help fuel your desire to accomplish even more.

You're the only one who will really
know whether you made the effort to
do the best of what you're capable.
John Wooden
Legendary UCLA Basketball Coach

CHAPTER
2

Goal Setting – The Next Step

Do the common uncommonly well.

Harvey Mackay

Beware the Naked Man Who Offers You His Shirt

Goal Setting – The Next Step

In the previous chapter you read about all the hurdles that prevent you from realizing your full potential. In this chapter, you will be shown that with desire, the decision to take action, the discipline to change your behavior, and determination, you'll get a lot more out of life. By establishing goals you accept responsibility for your own future.

Legend has it that Walt Disney planned out every detail of Disney World from the location of popcorn stands to the colors of storefronts. He had his vision and focused his goal-setting objectives on that vision.

Through the measuring of our progress toward our established goals we can determine the areas of life where we're successful and what areas of our life need improvement.

John Wooden, the legendary basketball coach, said: "Don't measure yourself by what you have accomplished, but by what you should have accomplished with your ability." Through goal-setting we push ourselves to the level Mr. Wooden suggests. Goals provide you with a structure for your life. Without goals our decisions can become inconsistent.

When we dream we never dream to have less (quality or quantity) than we currently have. The same is true with goal setting. We can push ourselves to the next level by establishing challenging goals.

If you don't have a goal for reaching your dream that you can describe in a sentence, you really don't know where you're going. We've all seen the posters and heard the phrase: if you don't know where you're going, any road will get you there. Establishing goals that can be verbalized in a short statement is the first step in finding the correct path to realizing your dreams.

What can goals help us to achieve?

- Clear goals help us set high standards for ourselves, in all areas of our lives.
- Through goal setting we take responsibility for our own destiny.
- Goals focus us on what we want to do or to become.

Goals don't necessarily need to be written, but it sure helps! Some goals are so imbedded in our mind we might ask ourselves, why write them down? A possible answer is, why not? A great answer is: the mental excitement you'll receive from actually crossing the goal off your list when it is accomplished speaks for itself.

Writing helps the idea (dream) go from head to paper; it helps us to chisel the goal in stone.

Keep in mind your goals must meet the following criteria:

They must be specific and measurable.

They must be realistic and attainable, yet challenging.

They must have a target date or timetable.

An acquaintance of mine set a goal for herself of getting her MBA (a goal) in a two-year (a target date) time, (measurable) and graduating with a GPA of 3.5 or higher (measurable). Now, look at this goal: specific, measurable, attainable, challenging and all of this with a target date.

I'm sure I don't need to inform you that Yes, all of this was accomplished!

In the process of measuring ourselves, meeting goals is paramount. The process of meeting your goals through measuring yourself is a secondary outcome, not to be overlooked.

To help us handle all the different situations life throws at us, we need goals. They serve as guidelines; with goals our decisions are not random but well thought-out. With goals we don't do anything haphazard. Do we need goals for everything? The answer is no, but we need them for everything we want to accomplish. Goal setting eliminates procrastination. The accomplishment of goals leads to a more productive life. The procrastinator experiences what could have been but wasn't.

Most people don't have a personal definition of success. Without one, you will never know if you *are* a success. **Take the time to define success, set the goals (measurable) that you want to reach, and begin the journey.**

Choosing a personal definition of success is not easy, mainly because there are so many parts of our lives we need to work on. Goals should cover all aspects of ourselves in order for us to become well-rounded. These should include examining areas such as: financial, spiritual, physical, career and family.

Through the evaluation of our values we establish what goals to assign to each area. One person may put more emphasis on physical over career, or financial over family. As long as we stay within our own value system we'll remain true to ourselves. Keep in mind, life is an ever-changing journey. What may be a personal priority this year may not be the top priority next year.

There are four steps to realizing goals:

1. Determine your goals and set attainable objectives.
2. Identify the steps to attaining your goals and plan when to take them.
3. Be willing to *do*, and dedicate the time that's necessary to reach your goals.
4. Take action and stick to your plan's deadline until it's complete.

Do something – anything - toward accomplishing your goals. Momentum has a powerful way of working on the human spirit.

Most people don't fail from lack of talent, money, or even desire. Most fail because they quit too soon. The business world is full of individuals who didn't get that last promotion or big assignment and internally quit. They didn't have the nerve to go to their boss and actually hand in a resignation letter, but mentally they quit. The individuals who get ahead in their careers are those who do a self-evaluation regarding why they didn't get the assignment or promotion, they work on these areas, and they're ready for the next opportunity.

If you chase two rabbits at the same time, you will probably end up with none. The same can be said about your goals. The goals you set need to be as specific as possible. Having a specific goal also makes it easier to realize when it's been accomplished. A lot can be said for written goals; pale ink is better than the best memory!

After establishing a goal, ask yourself: "Am I doing things right?" Then you must ask yourself, "Am I doing the right things?" If the answer is no, change your goal immediately!

In your career, personal goal setting and accomplishment should be considered mandatory. No one is going to help you advance your career or care more about your future than you. No matter what stage of your career you're in, whether new hire, management, or executive, you need goals and you need to continually measure yourself if you want to advance. Goals can include the areas of responsibility or pay or benefits.

Like my friend who obtained her MBA later in life, that was just one step in her journey. She then used this advanced degree to open new doors, resulting in her dream job.

Great companies today are looking for employees to enter into employment agreements whereby the company will give the individual an opportunity. The individual must then take some of the responsibility for learning what it takes to get the most for both the company and themselves, out of the opportunity.

Employment has a strange way of changing, like a chameleon. One quarter we might be in a time of high unemployment, with a lot of individuals looking for work. During these times businesses have their pick from a large group from the labor market. The next quarter business could be booming, unemployment is low and businesses have to do everything they can to keep their people.

Those who have goals and are continuously measuring themselves are comfortable in either situation of high or low employment. In times of high unemployment they are usually looked at as the best producers and they would only be let go if the company were closing. They most likely are also sought after by other companies for their high productivity.

In times of low unemployment with a lot of businesses putting out the "will hire" sign, these are the individuals sought out to open new divisions or branches. Those who measure themselves are the ones at the social gathering who are *not* talking about having made it through another round of layoffs, but are talking about their next big project.

The next time you hear yourself
saying,
"I'm just no good at...Ask yourself,
"Why Not?"

Marshall Goldsmith

What Got You Here Won't Get You There

In life there really is no reward for trying, only for achieving. Goals establish the paths to accomplish things and earn the accompanying rewards. Growing up we're told by our elders: try harder, try harder... the little engine that could. What we really needed to hear was: this is precisely what you're doing wrong; try it this way.

Success in life will come to those who consistently accomplish their goals and immediately establish new ones. What you must realize from the very start is that there is no end to goal setting or measuring yourself if you want to reach your full potential.

Fortunately for individuals measuring themselves and accomplishing goals, success begets success. You will notice as you start to accomplish your goals you will become very passionate about getting the important things done.

Individuals who have mastered goal setting and accomplishment techniques are the ones who in the future look back and say, "Look at what I accomplished!" This feeling of accomplishment is addictive-but what a great addiction to have.

Why do some people die soon after they retire? Abe Lincoln said, "Most people are about as happy as they make up their minds to be." You only need to visit Florida or Arizona to notice who the most vibrant and happy retirees are. They are the ones with goals; they're constantly measuring themselves.

What follows is a typical day in the life of two individual seniors. The first man: Church by 8 a.m., to the coffeehouse to meet friends by 9. Nine holes of golf at 10:30, need to break 55. If under 55, he asks himself why? Lunch at 1:00, two errands after lunch. Nap at 3:30, 30 minutes only; 4:15 outside for gardening; showers by 5:30, walks to the clubhouse to meet friends for 6:00 senior citizens' discount dinner. Laughs with his friends all through dinner because he got so much accomplished today. Home by 8, reads the paper, calls the kids and grandkids, to bed by 9:30.

Then there's the other man. It's too hot; I don't want to go out. The traffic is too busy; I don't want to drive. My golf clubs are old; I don't like to play with outdated equipment. I can't garden; it hurts my knees. I don't want to go out to eat; the food is never prepared the way I like it. I don't have time to clean the house today.

You can see why the former individual is destined for a long, happy life.

The very best proof that something can be done is the fact that others have already done it.

Brian Tracy

Focal Point

People who measure themselves don't necessarily have superior talent in any area other than in the area of goal setting. Examples of this are everywhere. In most of the professional golf tournaments the skill level of competitors is very close to the same: 300-yard drives, 9 irons within 5 feet of the hole. However, the golfer who generally wins the tournament is the player who has methodically laid out the course with a plan as to exactly which holes will be eagled, birdied or just par.

In the business world you see the same situations: the professional who got promoted to the 14th floor or the corner window office is the one who set his or her goals to get there and established plans to accomplish the steps it took to reach them.

These achievers manage their performance, upgrade their skills and plan their career. They know that all tasks can be accomplished one step at a time. Individuals who take the time to measure themselves have three traits in common: a positive attitude, persistence, and tenacity. What top achievers have in common is attitude. Don't ever let your attitude drift!

Believe in your ability to succeed, commit to doing your best and the results will speak for themselves. Why are successful people considered lucky? Because they make their own luck. They have put themselves into a position of responding a certain way when an opportunity presents itself. They have taken classes, visited a library, or gone to the practice range. They are always looking for ways to better themselves, so they truly are prepared when opportunity knocks.

All individuals attempting to achieve their objectives suffer setbacks. What if you get knocked down? There is no shame in getting knocked down as long as you learn from the experience so that the same event doesn't deter you in the future.

Successful people are very self-disciplined. As you accomplish more of your personal goals, the problems that might have posed a major roadblock to you in the past, you are now ready to attack-you've prepared yourself for those hurdles.

Goal setters learn that what not to do is sometimes more important than learning what to do.

Goals setters get everything out of life that is offered. They're constantly learning. They learn from accomplishing their goals and they learn from everything good and bad that gets in their way. They then use this information to accomplish other goals. They study other goals setters; they don't just admire others but they *study* them to help themselves.

This learning, growing and extending yourself turns out to be the real payoff from goal achievement.

You have to expect things of
yourself before you can do them.

Michael Jordan

Basketball Legend

CHAPTER

3

Set Goals That Are Measurable

Set Goals That Are Measurable

Highly successful people take a specific, and focused, approach to accomplishing their goals.

The starting point for full potential is clear goals:

1. These goals must be specific and measurable.
2. These goals must be believable and achievable.
3. These goals must be written out and time bound.

If it's not measurable, how will you know when you've accomplished it? Success (whatever your definition might be) begins with making your goals measurable. Then you can chart your progress. You will accomplish things that you measure because with a measurement you can manage!

In your quest to become a goal accomplisher, you're going to find that goals come in all sizes, time frames and levels of sophistication.

To merely state "I want to lose weight" allows you to say a two-pound decrease is considered an accomplishment of your goal. What you should have said is this: "Research shows a person of my size should weigh 165 pounds. I'm currently 185, hence my goal is to lose 20 pounds, or five pounds per month."

To state "I want to become a better business professional" is arbitrary and vague.

To state "I want to become a manager of my division
within 24 months" gives you direction.

By the yard it's hard
but inch by inch,
anything's a cinch.

Author Unknown

We measure everything, so why don't we reduce our goals to measurable steps (sub-goals) to realize them? Goals with measurements create motivation. Motivating ourselves is the best. Motivation by others normally does not last very long.

It's all in measuring! If you run into a goal that you're having trouble accomplishing, break it into smaller increments. The way you accomplish your major goals is by accomplishing smaller ones — sometimes you will need to break down even the smaller goals.

Years ago college graduates would search out the companies that offered the best management trainee programs. Their first measurable goal after obtaining a job with one of these companies was to receive a passing grade in the training program.

Having trouble assigning a measurement to your achievements? Ask yourself: "Why am I doing what I'm doing?" The answer to this question will be a measurement. **The more specific the goal, the easier it will be to measure and the better you will be able to visualize it in your mind.**

We need to establish challenging goals. Most people generally won't perform above their own or others' expectations. Knowing this, we need to set high expectations for ourselves and let our minds excel.

I believe strongly in the 80/20 Rule (Pareto's Law). Try to set goals that you have an 80 percent chance of accomplishing. If it's more than 80 percent it may end up being perceived as unattainable or unrealistic, leading to a demoralizing defeat.

If you believe you've set a goal that is not 80 percent achievable, break that goal down into smaller attainable goals. Your motivation level will soar.

The trick here is to remember through the accomplishment of small goals you are in fact putting the building blocks in place to accomplish your ultimate goals. Your goal to earn your MBA is very admirable; it begins with the registration for your first class and the accumulation of the credit hours.

Accomplishing small goals equates to small steps forward, which helps eliminate the possibility of being overwhelmed.

It's what you accomplish that determines your level of success. Setting goals, accomplishing these goals and setting new ones *is* what keeps you moving forward. To be as effective as possible in your private and professional life, you need to eliminate those activities that don't contribute to helping you accomplish your goals.

Make a plan to realize completion. This plan will allow you to determine where you are now, in real time. If you know where you are and where you want to be, you can then pick the shortest distance between the two.

Goal Setters: The future isn't something that happens to them; it happens because of them.

Michael W. Hill

April Heinrich, head soccer coach of the 2004 U.S. Women's National Team, had her players focus on the 99-1 ratio. April had her team concentrate 99 percent of their effort on the things they could control.

This same philosophy can be applied to a businessperson and his or her individual goals. Concentrate 99 percent of your effort on those things in your control, your personal education, your presentation skills, your interpersonal skills and your own mental attitude. You can't control the outcome, but as Ms. Heinrich states, "There's a great deal you can control in the process ahead of time that helps determine the outcome."

Nothing good happens by accident.

Peter Drucker
Author, Management Consultant

To reach your dreams you must list, in succession, the goals that will get you to the level you desire. Assign a deadline to each goal. This will help keep you focused.

Having listed each goal in succession, write a short sentence stating the action you are initially going to take to accomplish it. Each goal should now be viewed from a measurement perspective. If you cannot assign measurable actions to the goal, re-evaluate the goal. Assign measurements that make you happy, and proceed. Don't worry about what others think. You're the one who defines your success. Use others' opinions about how to accomplish a task but don't arbitrarily pick someone else's goal as yours.

I met an attorney who relayed to me his "career" story. Right out of law school he began practicing in a large firm. He had a couple of clearly defined goals: #1 Build up his practice whereby he would earn $100,000 a year and #2, earn partner status within the firm.

Well, on his way to becoming partner he passed the $100,000 a year goal but he realized his goal to become a partner was not what he truly wanted. So, he changed his goal. He decided to find three associates and start his own firm. Others in the practice of law might think that he failed to make partner, but no – he found that the big firm atmosphere was not for him so he became a "partner" in his own small firm.

The key to setting goals is not making them too easy or too hard. If they're too easy, we're really not pushing ourselves to our best ability. If we set them too high, we become disappointed and frustrated when we don't accomplish them.

Here are some hints: be honest with yourself. No one knows your limits or capabilities better than you do. Review your prior accomplishments: Do your current goals exceed what you've accomplished before? Review what your colleagues are doing. Are they outperforming you? Observe their habits and establish new ones for yourself. Habits are everything! They can make us unbelievably successful or they can lead us to becoming mediocre. Develop good habits as early in your career as you can.

If you're accomplishing the same goals as your colleagues, the measurement shows you're not getting ahead, you're just staying even.

Many of the management trainees I mentioned earlier didn't realize why they didn't get the promotion they expected when they finished the company-sponsored training program. The promotion always goes to that individual who does more than the rest. The individual who goes through the training and then does that "something extra" is the who is recognized at promotion time. The ones who take what they have learned and show management they can implement the knowledge – they're the ones who get ahead.

Short-term goals are normally considered anything less than three years, long-term are three or more. You should be able to list both short-term and long-term goals in all areas of your life-personal, professional, and spiritual.

What's broken, fix. If you run into a temporary setback, address the issue now. Don't put it off. Generally things we put off lead to other problems. Here's an example: You are taking an accounting class in order to earn your MBA. This class takes daily attention. You find on Wednesday you haven't opened your book yet this week! The goal is a daily review of the lesson plan. Don't tell yourself you'll work extra hard on the weekend. By delaying your work, you have over-booked your weekend.

Let's look at another example: I know of a saleslady whose financial goal for the year is to earn $50,000. Most sales people who have goals like this get to September or October of the year, find out they're on track to only make $35,000, and give up. They end up putting their dream off until next year.

Not this sales professional. She had broken down her goal into smaller goals: $1,000 per week (she's factored in a two-week vacation) or $200 per day. Daily she tracks her sales and she knows what sale that day puts her at or over her number. When Friday rolls around she sometimes hits her $1,000 weekly goal with her first sale after lunch. This allows her to accomplish another goal she has set for herself: to spend more time with her children. Imagine how excited the kids are to see mom come to pick them up a few hours early. She doesn't let the mañana syndrome (putting everything off until tomorrow) affect her plans.

Let me summarize this chapter:
   Goals must be *clear*. You must be able to articulate them.

Give yourself a precise, goal-oriented agenda.
Determine how much time a task will take and don't
overbook yourself.
Evaluate where you stand-at all times and at each
stage you should know where you are in accomplishing a goal.

CHAPTER

4

Measuring Your Progress And Rewarding Yourself

Measure success by success,
not by the number of failures
it takes to achieve it.

Harvey Mackay

Measuring Your Progress And Rewarding Yourself

How do we measure ourselves? Some people use a GANTT chart. This is an elaborate system used by the United States Army to visually show scheduled and actual progress of a project. The chart accurately tracks progress on different tasks, and identifies those that need to be accomplished before the ultimate task can be considered complete. This is an excellent old-world tool even by today's standards for project management.

The tactic to verify you are moving forward is to continually analyze your goals and performance to assure yourself you have not become stagnant — or worst-case scenario, losing ground. The world currently moves at such a fast pace that if you're not moving forward, you *are* losing ground.

The ongoing process of measuring yourself and your progress toward your goals is very self-serving. The more you focus on your goals the more your desire to achieve them grows. The stronger your passion, the faster you'll want to accomplish each step.

Successful individuals have very low alibi thresholds, both for themselves and for others. To get past an excuse, go back to your motive! Re-evaluate your reasons behind setting the goal in the first place, then re-define the steps you chose to get there.

By thinking backward from your goal you can create a roadmap to travel forward to get you there. I once worked with a guy who confided in me his desire to own a manufacturer's rep agency. After a few conversations I was really surprised how much this individual had broken down his goals into sub-goals. First, he knew exactly how much money was needed and how long at his present rate of savings it would take him to amass that amount. He didn't like the time frame so he took on a second job to speed up his savings rate. He knew he would need some additional business knowledge so he began taking one of three classes he had identified to increase his acumen in those fields.

You need to take ownership of your own situation. If you don't do it no one else will do it for you.

Make sure all the sub-goals you're working toward accomplishing are essential to your ultimate goals. Magic Johnson has 6 NBA Championships, 3 MVPs, and 1 Olympic gold medal. His coaches told him to envision each game as a step toward winning a championship.

Each long-term goal must be supported by short-term or sub-goals. The short-term goals provide the path or track to help you eventually obtain your long-range goals. While working on the short-term goals, you need to measure your progress. If you find that you are scoring little successes, great! Proceed to your next goal. However, if during an evaluation you find you are not measuring up, try breaking down that goal into smaller ones. The accomplishment of the little successes is very important. It keeps you moving toward your ultimate goal and it helps you mentally to maintain a high level of confidence, motivation and enthusiasm. **You'll never see anyone frown after accomplishing a personal goal.**

How did professional basketball player Michael Jordan average 30 points a game for 10 years? The answer: eight points per quarter! He knew that if he could score eight points a quarter (a short-term goal) his long-term goal of 30+ points per game would be accomplished. He of course also realized that his performance would motivate the other players and the ultimate goal, winning the game, would be a sure bet.

The only way to know how
your day is going is to keep score.

Harvey Mackay

Dig Your Well Before You're Thirsty

During your journey you will run into people who attempt to degrade you and your ideas, or even insult your goals. Look at this for what it truly is: in attempting to discourage you, they seek to elevate themselves by comparison. In real life it doesn't work that way—you elevate yourself through hard work and accomplishments.

Some scholars believe that the roots of disappointment and guilt lie in our failure to pursue our potential. All our personal rewards do not have to be tangible items. The feeling of knowing that a goal has been accomplished is most gratifying. The individuals you run into in life who are most disappointed with their lives are those without goals.

Paul Stoltz, in his book *Adversity Quotient at Work,* describes three types of employees; quitters are those people who retired years ago but just never bothered to tell anyone. Campers is the term Paul uses to describe those individuals who get the job done sufficiently, they simply don't strive as hard or sacrifice as much as they once did. Then there are the climbers-those individuals dedicated to a lifelong ascent. They make things happen; they are tenacious and refuse to accept defeat for long.

No matter what type of industry you're in, organizations in one way or another, formally or informally rank their employees. Your goal is to be ranked in the top 10 percent. Become an "A" player, a climber.

GE became famous during the Jack Welch years as a company that "ranked and yanked." This term referred to the GE practice of ranking their employees top to bottom in each department and then systematically letting the bottom 10 percent go. **There are consequences for underperformers!**

Never cease trying to be
the best you can become.

John Wooden

People without goals are like boats without rudders. They think they're making progress in one direction only to have a strong wind come up and blow them back farther than where they started, or in an entirely different direction.

A recession shows you exactly what happens to the employees without personal business goals. They're the first ones let go when the company hits rough water.

People who set goals and measure themselves are like boats with rudders and the newest GPS (global positioning system). They have a good steering mechanism and map to keep them in line with their destination-accurately and timely.

If you find yourself not making the progress you had hoped for, re-evaluate. Try to define your goal in the clearest terms possible. What are you willing to do to reach the desired target? By re-establishing your thoughts toward your goal, you'll find added motivation. You need to be clear about why you are doing what you are doing.

One way to accomplish anything is to study an expert. Find someone who has accomplished what you want to accomplish and investigate how he or she did it. In some cases this may lead you to a mentor relationship. Most successful people are more than willing to share their secrets to success. In most cases you'll find their methods can be broken down into an event or series of events that will help you follow the right path to achievement.

Let's take a look at a couple of examples. Lee Iacocca is one of the country's most famous and successful automobile executives. When asked how he became so successful he stated that he really studied the automobile industry. By studied I'm sure he meant: read books and articles, listened to engineers, and paid attention to marketing surveys. Mr. Iacocca also spent many years working in different managerial positions to get a wealth of personal experience.

Now let's look at Michael Dell, of Dell Computers. Michael took a different approach than Mr. Iacocca's. He studied the customers. Beginning in college he would actually go to the students' (customers') dorm rooms and ask them what they wanted in their computer, then he would go and make it. Mr. Dell took the time to study the wants and needs of the customers and then went about setting up the company structure to service that demand.

- Be aware of "analysis paralysis," or trying to analyze a situation too much.
- Always evaluate your failures. It's not the failure, but what you learn from it, that counts. If you don't examine the reasons "why," it's likely you'll repeat the same mistakes.
- Most people crave attention and recognition. When we are accomplishing something for someone else, the reward and recognition are often obvious. The boss says, "If you do 'x' for the company, the company will give you 'y' in return."

When you're attempting to complete goals that only *you* are aware of, you need to find ways to show self-appreciation. A good way to pat yourself on the back is to give yourself an award. It could be anything you value: clothing, nice meals, travel, electronic gadgets. These can all act as motivators to keep you headed up the achievement path. This reward should be commensurate with the goal you've just accomplished. Continually celebrate your victories.

Be realistic. If your goal is to earn a big salary, you will need to work for an organization that pays big salaries. Don't set a goal for yourself of a three handicap in golf if you live in an area where because of the weather you can only play four months of the year, or because of family commitments you can only play once a month.

Think about pro golfers. Private jets, caddies, luxury hotels, fitness trainers, you name it and the top golfers get it-most of the time at the click of their fingers.

Now, consider their personal evaluation system: every Thursday, Friday, Saturday, and Sunday their performance is posted for the entire world to see, in the form of scores. Think of how much more we could get done and the quality of our work if we knew that our performance was going to be posted for all to see.

Continually measure your situation and yourself.

Michael W. Hill

Another advantage of a reward system is that it keeps your enthusiasm strong. Nothing great was ever achieved without enthusiasm. Keep your level of drive high. Rewards can do just that.

Most people assume that rewards are only motivating if someone else gives them to you. This is not true; a reward we give ourselves can be just as powerful-possibly more so, because we know what kind of reward we truly want. Rewards are the most effective way to develop new habits. Just don't get carried away. Always make sure the level of the reward is in line with the level of the accomplishment.

When you need motivation, here are a few techniques you can use to help keep you on track:

- Post a picture of your reward with a description of your goal. You'll begin to associate one with the other and it will act as a continuous reminder that you're working on the particular goal for a reason.
- Celebrate ALL accomplishments. As long as you're accomplishing any goal, you're moving in the right direction.
- Find someone else who has had the same goal and accomplished it. The very best proof that something can be done is the fact that another person has already done it.
- Announce your intentions to others. You can normally shrug off a lack of accomplishment if you've only made the commitment to yourself with a quick "missed it," or "got too busy." To admit it to others is a lot tougher, and it's embarrassing.

CHAPTER

5

What We Measure, We Can Improve

We live in a performance-oriented society.
Put up or shut up.
Put out or get out.
The pressure to perform is enormous.

Lawrence Boldt

How to Be, Do, or Have Anything

What We Measure, We Can Improve

Measure, measure, measure! We measure everything: the time it takes to get to work, what our child's high school grade point average is, the amount of money we have in our 401(k) plan. We measure everything — but what most people don't do is react to the measurements.

An average employee will say: "It takes me 20 minutes to get to work. I need to be at my desk at 8:00, so I'll leave home at 7:40." These employees are the ones we normally see sitting down at their desk at 8:05, 8:10 or 8:30, because something happened on the way to work. Rain, snow, or "I didn't hit all the lights like I usually do."

Have you ever heard of the promotion going to the individual who has his or her MBA, has good experience, generates good ideas and is only a few minutes late each day? No, of course not. The successful individuals are those who measure themselves, evaluate their measurements and react to them. In our example, it takes 20 minutes to get to the office in good weather; so add some time for bad weather, construction or that complete range of unexpected problems that can arise.

What we measure we can improve! If we don't measure we have no starting point, average, or personal best. With a measurement we have a gauge with which we can evaluate *why* it is, *what* it is, and make adjustments to it — our performance.

Think backwards through the steps to figure out how to work in small increments, one simple behavior change at a time.

Obviously, the steps you go through to improve must be measurable. Remember; if you can't measure it you can't improve it. When you have identified the measurable steps you need to find a standard to judge yourself against.

Use either past successful performers or the competition–both are worthy standards to gauge your performance.

How did Roger Bannister elevate himself to break the four-minute mile barrier? He set aside time every day to train, to measure his progress, to evaluate, and train some more. His result: May 6, 1954, he became the first man to run a sub-four-minute mile.

In goal accomplishment, you are measured by your outcomes and achievements rather than your motives or activities. When attempting to achieve one of your goals it makes no difference if you spend 10 minutes or 10 days; what you want is achievement of the goal and then you can set new ones.

When you take a look at a measurement you want to improve, be sure to do so with an open mind. You're looking for any opportunity to improve your performance. Optimism begets success because you welcome all possibilities. The optimist knows that even if the steps toward success are very small they will ultimately lead to accomplishments.

Evaluate your progress from this perspective: are you moving forward in your quest? Remember, if you continue to do what you've always done, you'll continue to get the results you've always gotten. If you have reached a plateau or even a slight decline, evaluate your actions–physical and mental.

There are many things to be gained from measurements. The two most helpful are: to compare yourself to others and to compare yourself to a previous personal achievement.

When Benjamin Franklin decided he wanted to become proficient at writing, he first had his work critiqued. He then found examples of writings clearly superior to his own, and then he devised his own system to make himself better. Daily he would do some writing, self-evaluate it and then re-write.

What makes Franklin's accomplishment so outstanding was his determination. He practiced his writing while holding a job in the printing industry, so he wrote before work in the morning, after work at night and on Sundays.

How many of us have the determination to design our own self-improvement program-a program designed to discover our faults, and then work on correcting these faults while working at our regular job, managing home and family, and balancing other responsibilities?

From Franklin's plan we can learn a few key points:

- You must know what you want.
- You must design a system for improvement and self-evaluation.
- You must be dedicated to transforming old habits to new habits with better payoffs.

Only the mediocre are
always at their best.

Jean Giraudoux (1882–1944)

Diplomat and writer

When Pat Riley took over coaching the Los Angeles Lakers, he faced the ultimate challenge: how to motivate a team that had just won the NBA Championship. Most of these men had reached the pinnacle of their life's dreams, to be recognized as the "best" and to be receiving compensation at a level most people cannot even relate to.

How did Mr. Riley motivate these champions? He evoked the "one percent more" performance request. If everyone on the team could improve his individual statistics by one percent, they could repeat as NBA Champions. The Lakers did go on to win the Championship that year with many individual team members setting career high achievement marks.

Look at the keys to Mr. Riley's tactics. Establish a benchmark: at what level are you currently performing? Add one percent to it! When setting your goals, don't downplay your current level of success. Set goals that are challenging and set measurements in place to meet or exceed your expectations. Most people will perform up to their level of expectations.

Improvement can be exhilarating when it's an outcome of the evaluation system.

A friend of mine is trying to become the best golfer he can be. He has identified that goal with a measurement, which is a handicap of eight on the USGA rating system. Why an eight? He has figured it puts him in a very unique group of golfers. Any higher number and he feels he won't stand out, and any lower number will take too much practice and keep him from other goals in his life. This friend is an excellent sand trap player—just like the pros. How often does he practice his sand shots? Not very often. It's a skill he has mastered, so he practices enough to keep it sharp, but he instead focuses on weaker areas of his golf game and sets goals for each.

Once you have reached a measurement level you're satisfied with, move on to another goal. Perfection in one area can drain your energy from other endeavors.

General Douglas MacArthur defined
success as the ability to produce.

It is believed that artist Leonardo da Vinci worked on the Mona Lisa for four years and was still working on it and trying to improve it until his death.

I personally believe the Mona Lisa is a masterpiece, and I'm disappointed that da Vinci didn't feel the same way and spend more time creating more masterpieces, rather than obsessing over the Mona Lisa.

In the business world you're paid for results, not activities— you're also paid to do your work to a certain acceptable quality level. I'm sure we all know the employee who when they're asked to perform a task they do 50 percent more-thinking this will catch management's attention and result in additional praise, maybe a raise, or possibly a promotion.

Most of the time management is looking for that individual who does a 100 percent job and then is able to start on the next project. Make sure you're showing results, not just activity!

To accomplish goals, you need to be very honest with yourself and give yourself a very truthful evaluation. You may need to change things in your life to get what you really want. If your goal is to have an income of $75,000 a year and the president of the company only makes $100,000, you need a reality check. It may mean leaving that company or industry, or finding a second source of income.

Your goals need to be consistent with your physical and mental limitations. Nothing is more stifling than shooting for something that is unattainable. Work within your means.

Only 2 percent of college basketball players ever go on to play professionally. However, when you ask the senior-level players, most state they believe they are professional material. This is not realistic. They can dream but they also need to set more attainable and realistic goals.

As kids growing up we were always told, "Learn from your mistakes." What a great recommendation. I propose an even better recommendation: learn from the mistakes of others. Then, you don't have to waste your time making the mistake in the first place.

One way to achieve your goals is to emulate the performance of those who have already achieved what you're after. Who makes the best coaches? Those athletes who have experienced the difficulties and challenges of competition and have mastered the management skills of coaching.

To achieve goals it takes patience, discipline and effort. Not always in equal amounts.

How do you go about changing? Here are some helpful tips: Change your attitude. Your attitude affects everything you do. It can also affect everybody around you. You can choose to be around optimistic or pessimistic individuals. Which do you prefer to associate with? What type of people do you prefer to attract into your life?

Create a new plan. If you are not achieving what you're going after, take a step back, evaluate, organize, and execute a new plan. Reading one management book every six months to improve your business skills may not be helping you improve. You may need to read one book a month. Evaluate the amount of time you are dedicating to accomplishing what you've set out to do.

Even if you are No.1,
you can't stay at the
top of the heap if you
don't continually improve.

Author Unknown

Don't assume Lady Luck will pull you through to goal accomplishment. Who are the luckiest people you know? More than likely they are the ones who work the hardest and are the ones ready when the moment of opportunity presents itself.

Let's assume you think you are doing everything in your power to accomplish a goal and you've failed. Don't waste your time focusing on the fact that you failed, but focus on the reasons why. Examining these reasons will keep you from failing again.

The reasons for failure are countless. You may need to really probe for the answers. This may take a lot of soul searching. Don't be afraid to ask yourself the difficult questions and lay out a game plan for change. When posed with a problem you cannot personally find an answer to, ask for help! Find an expert, a mentor, or maybe even a coach, depending on the nature of your problem.

CHAPTER
6

Fire The Boss

Fire The Boss

By practicing the techniques and recommendations in this book you will become a top performer, and others will be noticing!

Let's say you have turned yourself into a goal setting and accomplishing individual. In your professional career this will more than likely bring you to a crossroad.

Nine out of ten people say they are more productive when they're around positive people.

Tom Rath, Donald Clifton

How Full Is Your Bucket?

You will notice that winners and accomplishers tend to associate with other winners and accomplishers. Do you want to grind away at a job where the group doesn't click because the 80/20 rule is in place? (Twenty percent of the employees are doing 80 percent of the work.) Or do you want to seek out that situation where you're working with a group of high performers? When you're a top performer and you work with top performers, job satisfaction climbs. Jobs and positions are more secure in a company of top performers. Finally, top performers in top organizations get paid more.

Life is not always fair.

John Kennedy

35th President of the United States of America

What about the boss who refuses to recognize or praise your good work and maybe even discourages rather than encourages your development? Fire the boss! If the company you're with is a top performer and you're being stifled, there are two choices: continue to perform at the highest level you can, given the circumstances, and hope to be noticed by others, or you can choose to leave. If you choose to stay, possibly there are others in the organization looking for assistance in a particular area and you would be a good fit, or possibly a division transfer is possible. In the business world we don't talk a lot about networking within our own companies, but we should.

Differentiating yourself is the key to your success. There are many ways to differentiate yourself. Become the idea guy, the best manager, the highest-producing salesperson. Find your passion and use it.

You always look where there's
change. Change is what
creates opportunity.

Gary Wendt
Former CEO of Conseco

There's nothing more disappointing than when you're not recognized for your accomplishments.

Let's assume you've turned yourself into a top performer and you're not getting the credit you deserve. Bosses generally don't want to be upstaged. Some see subordinates' promotions as embarrassing! Actually, the smart boss can take one of two positions when a subordinate is a top performer. One position is to take credit for grooming a competent employee. A second position is for the boss to challenge himself or herself, set goals and elevate his or her performance to surpass the level of the subordinate.

Are you working *for* or *with* your boss? After some careful situation evaluation, if you find you're working "for" a boss, it's time for a change! A boss you work "for" is looking for subordinates to be robots with minimal or no interaction. A boss you work "with" understands the value of human capital. Great bosses realize the employees hold the key to a company's success. They care for and nurture the employees, and ask for their input.

Don't sit there patiently waiting for something to happen. The worst thing you can do is to mentally quit and then not take any proactive steps to improve your situation. Even though you may not be *the* boss, you are *your own* boss. Put your own business plan together.

The future belongs to
the competent.

Brian Tracy
Author, Professional speaker

Don't wait on the boss to evaluate your performance (more on this later). I recently met with a lady who had been put on a 90-day probationary period. She had been told that if she did not meet certain goals within 90 days she would be terminated. She went on to inform me that the day we were talking was day 70. I asked her how she was doing, She said on one of the three goals, she had already accomplished what the boss wanted. On the second goal she was on pace to have it completed within the 90 days and on the third—she "thought' she was doing what the boss wanted but wasn't sure. My recommendation was to get with the boss immediately and get the confusion cleared up. She was so intimidated by this boss that she wanted to not "bother' her until the 90-day review.

Well, I'm happy to report she did meet with her boss and the boss was so impressed with her progress on the first two goals they had a lengthy discussion about what was really needed to accomplish the third goal and the boss gave my friend an additional 90 days to get it accomplished.

In my first book: ***Measuring to Manage*** I describe how companies think nothing of spending countless dollars each year formulating the business plan that will take them to the "next" level. The best companies evaluate their employees and develop strategies to push them to a higher tier of responsibility.

What you need to do, as an individual attempting to achieve personal goals, is start clarifying your future, with targets such as: sales manager in three years, vice president in ten. Goals like this can be accomplished when you put the plan, process, and attitude in place.

Learn from your past and current bosses. Take the time to recognize and record the good management traits of each and the poor traits. Learning from other's mistakes is one of the fastest ways to succeed.

I'm always shocked when I hear how disappointed people are that their careers are not moving ahead as fast as they would like. They say, "I do everything the boss asks." Isn't everyone who gets to keep their jobs doing *everything they're asked to do*? Careers move forward when you do that *little bit more* than asked.

Another way to make yourself stand out is to be proactive in getting yourself into situations that show off your talents. Offer to head up a new project, lead a meeting, contribute at a convention. All are ways to showcase your worth. If one does not self-promote, one does not get promoted.

Change is essential if you are going to improve your situation. One thing is for certain: **If you just sit there doing what you've always done–you'll get what you've always gotten.**

Don't let job dissatisfaction become a norm. A continual problem in any area of life, if not brought under control, can quickly affect all other areas. Who wants to become labeled as negative and pessimistic? It's a hard label to change.

Optimism, however, is also a contagious trait. If you can get yourself truly happy in one area of your life, watch how your happiness and optimism spread to other areas.

CHAPTER

7

Realizing Our Full Potential
Is An Ongoing Process

Stay in the personal development business forever.

Bradford Smart

Topgrading

Realizing Our Full Potential
Is An Ongoing Process

Who are the people with goals seeking their full potential? They're the individuals at the top of any list. The top management of a company, the top of the leader board at Sunday's PGA tournament, the highest percentage pitchers, batters, quarterbacks...these are the top performers. You don't "fall" to the top of the mountain. You train, you practice, you study techniques, you set goals, measure yourself and then enjoy the summit view as you climb.

Look at the top performers in the business world. Most of the top managers have been with their company for many years. They have set personal goals for themselves and their divisions. They learned the techniques that helped them get the most out of themselves and others and this led to their advancement.

Goal setting and becoming an accomplisher are addicting, but what a great addiction to have!

It's just as easy to be addicted to a passive life where you wait for things to happen or to fall in your lap. So, pick the more respected and beneficial addiction and challenge yourself to get as much out of life as possible.

Let's look at sports figure Tiger Woods. It's reported that in the year 2007 Tiger made $22,000,000 from playing in golf tournaments and almost $100,000,000 through endorsements. I'm using 2007 because golfers will remember that Tiger missed most of 2008 while recovering from a surgery.

What keeps him practicing every day, exercising every day – putting himself through all the training? It sure can't be the money. Tiger is chasing history! It's an admirable target. His goal is: to win more "Majors" than anyone. His goal is to be the best and it sure would seem he has the personal formula to achieve it.

What happened at GE when Jack Welch announced his decision to retire? Three top executives were in the running for the open position! Each one, I'm sure, had his own plan and goal to become a CEO. Each one may not have had the same goal as Jeff Immelt–that goal of becoming the CEO of GE.

But, look at what happened when it was announced that Mr. Immelt would become the Jack Welch replacement. Each of the others left to become CEO of other Fortune 500 companies.

Was Jeff Immelt the only one totally focused on the CEO of GE position and the others were focused on CEO of "any" Fortune 500 company?

Your success and reputation are totally within your control. Make a personal decision to become a goal-setter and accomplisher, and back it up with plans. Start with a small goal and proceed to more complicated ones. The main point is to *start* the journey. Your life will change when others look at you as a doer rather than a dreamer.

Henry Ford said, "You can't build a reputation on what you're going to do."

It takes action! It takes measurable goals! It takes a plan of attack! Results are what counts.

Patrick Lencioni describes three signs of a miserable job: lack of measurement (if you can't measure what you are doing then you'll soon lose interest in it; irrelevance (the feeling that what you do at work has no impact on the lives of others; and anonymity (managers not taking an interest in their people).

If you're working for a manager who isn't addressing these three areas (all very measurable), you're in for one rough road. You can ride it out and hope that your manager either dies, gets fired, or quits. Then you have to hope the next boss is better. Or, you can leave. Look for that company and/or manager that addresses these areas, those managers who make it easy for employees to measure their progress.

As Lencioni says, "Employees who can measure their own progress or contributions are going to develop a greater sense of personal responsibility and satisfaction than those who can't."

The harsh reality is that if you're not
constantly moving forward,
you're losing professional ground.

Susan A. DePhillips

Author

I know examples of employees who have been in these types of situations and have ended up in great situations.

One friend was disappointed with the company he was working with because of a boss who failed to recognize his accomplishments and was always told "he could have done better." Well, the day he was going to turn in his resignation was the same day the corporation decided to terminate his boss. Fortunately for my friend he was going to resign after lunch and his boss was terminated in the morning.

Mr. Ford had to research parts for his automobiles, plan a manufacturing process, and decide on a distribution system, to realize his ultimate goal: "an automobile in every driveway." **You need to set plans in place to accomplish your goals. Write them down, make them specific, give them a completion date and identify action steps to achieve them.**

Studies show that those individuals who set goals in their life are those who accomplish the most. Lou Holtz, the collegiate football coach, stated that after he became a goal-setter he became a "participant" in life rather than a "spectator."

The answer is in the **first step**. The first step is so hard. There are always a million reasons not to get started, but through some careful soul searching you'll find *that one reason* that gets you motivated. *That one reason* that gets your heart pumping. Get your heart pumping and a funny thing happens: the rest of your body will follow.

Learn to have faith in yourself. If you're willing to put the time in to make yourself better, you're in the minority- a minority you want to be in! Most people just won't take the time to improve themselves. They won't read a book, take a class, find a mentor. The ones who do are the ones who become successful.

A good friend of mine wanted to put "public speaking" on his resume. A couple of years ago I was having lunch with him and he told me about one of his meetings with a professional speaker in Indianapolis. I was curious, so I asked, "How do you know him?" He got this almost embarrassed look on his face and replied, "One day I just got up the nerve and called him." He went on to tell me that he recognized Frank as a highly sought-after public speaker so he called and asked him if he might have time to have a cup of coffee. Well, that one cup of coffee led to a beautiful mentor-mentee situation that has helped my friend become an excellent public speaker himself.

Many people go through life reacting
to circumstances and events rather
than creating what happens.

Cyndi Crother

Catch!

Employees without goals are doomed to work for the employees with goals.

Become known in your company as an achiever, the one who puts that little bit extra into a project or task. The one who can find that extra time to accomplish a little bit more. The one who doesn't wait to be handed a project, but instead brings a concept or a new idea to the boss. These are the individuals destined to get ahead in a business environment.

Susan DePhillips, in *Corporate Confidential* explores the idea that those individuals truly trying to get ahead in the business world don't wait for their annual performance appraisals. Ms. DePhillips states that the smart professionals don't wait-they seek performance feedback continuously.

Be careful when asking co-workers for feedback, as sometimes the 80/20 rule applies: 80 percent don't care about your goals to be successful and 20 percent want to see you fail.

Your best possibility is to find a mentor to help you along or fellow businessmen and women outside your corporation. Many times these are the ones who will be most honest in evaluating your performance.

A friend of mine makes it a point every year at her industry's annual convention to set time aside to have a breakfast or lunch with her peers to review each other's progress toward their professional goals.

Your life gets better when you get better.

Brian Tracy
Focal Point

Continuous learning is another key to reaching your full potential. Whether it is through classes at a local community college, DVDs, seminars, or books at your local library, stay on the cutting edge of your industry or field.

In business you can't remain competitive if you're not learning as fast as your competition. The same is true of you as a growing individual. If you're learning and accomplishing the same goals as your associates, you're really not getting anywhere—you're standing still. I hope that through this book you realize you can accomplish so much more in life if you just push yourself that little bit.

There's only one way to coast, and that's downhill. In the business world there is no coasting, not for high-performance individuals and not for their companies. If you're coasting downhill, you can almost always be assured there's someone else pedaling downhill and they will always catch up to and pass the coaster.

While doing research for this book, one major finding that kept repeating itself was that the high achievers, the ones who separate themselves from the rest, are those who are self-motivated and constantly doing self-evaluations. Yes, for sure these individuals can turn it up a notch when there's a company-sponsored contest of some sort going on. In general they are always operating at a level above the rest. They have a self-motivation that focuses them on succeeding and they use that inner drive to elevate themselves above the rest.

Let's look at a sports example and a business example.

What motivates a businessperson who is making more money than they could ever possibly spend to continue the daily grind? I've found that it's an inner motivation to either do better than the previous vice-president, CEO or whomever, or it's to beat last quarter's or last year's numbers. These individuals have set their own goals and targets and motivate themselves to achieve them.

Lee Iacocca had a long tenure at the Ford Motor Company and financially he described himself as "set for life." His goal had always been to run the company—when he was passed over for the position he could have very easily retired to the good life, played golf, traveled, and done some volunteer work. But, no, he gets himself in the position to be offered the opportunity to run a competing car company, Chrysler.

Now some might say revenge motivated him to seek a position competing with the company that had "passed him over." But, revenge is only a short-term motivator. What pushes a man like Lee Iacocca is the inner drive to prove to himself that he could do what he always knew he could.

To earn more,
you must learn more.

Brian Tracy

Author

I'm sure by now you've realized the rewards go to those who accomplish, not to those who just try.

Many golfers try for a hole in one, but the beautiful trophy only goes to the one who actually sinks it. In business the promotion goes to the employee who accomplishes his or her assigned tasks, not the one who merely tries.

Need additional help in measuring yourself? Find a mentor; seek out experienced individuals in the areas you're trying to succeed in. Who doesn't love to be asked for advice? Many individuals get a real sense of accomplishment helping someone reach their goals. Don't be afraid to ask!

Nowadays businesspeople are even turning to personal coaches-the thought being if Tiger Woods, the #1 golfer in the world, needs a coach, shouldn't I have one, too?

What can coaches do? They can help you with aligning your priorities to be the best you can be. They'll offer good, solid feedback on ways to improve yourself, and they'll make sure your goals are measurable and written. They'll even help you develop a timeline for your business aspirations.

It's never too late to be
who you might have been.

Author Unknown

The world is full of successful people. To keep yourself on the path of realizing your full potential, study those people. Find those who have accomplished what you want to accomplish and mimic them. Most people merely admire those successful people. You can do more. The world has a funny way of helping along those individuals with a plan and a goal. Become a part of an elite group.

Imitate successful people's good habits. A habit by definition is: a constant, often unconscious inclination to perform some act, acquired through its frequent repetition.

With this in mind, pick and practice good habits. With repetition they may even become unconscious acts.

Thomas Jefferson said: "An investment in yourself is the best investment you can make."

The more talent you have,
The more valuable you are.

Harvey Mackay

Fired Up

You've been told whenever you find yourself with any discretionary income, put 10 percent in your 401(k) or IRA. Well, I would propose that you spend some of that money on yourself! Buy an educational book, take a class at the community college, subscribe to the latest business magazine.

To be successful in any situation, personal or business, you must first defeat laziness. You must replace your bad habits with good ones. Don't watch both football games on Sunday afternoon. Watch one and work on your personal business plan instead of watching the second.

Do something different than your co-workers are doing. Separate yourself from the crowd.

Occasionally take a step back and ask yourself, "What does success mean to me?" Success means different things to different people. Do you want to acquire a lot of personal possessions? Do you seek a fulfilling personal life but with minimal possessions? Do you strive for recognition and notoriety?

In your desire to reach your goals you'll run into setbacks. It could be negative people, or it could be goals set too high. These are the times you need to work harder on your process and bounce back. Stay calm, collect your thoughts and move ahead. You need to live day by day. **Learn from the past; expect the best in the future but concentrate on today's activities.**

Some of us sit back and wait to see what life is going to throw at us. Others take a look around at all the wonderful things life has to offer and make plans to experience as many of the wonders as possible.

If you're not passionate about what you're doing, your heart won't be in it.

Find career goals that get your heart
pumping.

Michael W. Hill

CHAPTER

8

"Your" Performance Evaluation

Don't wait on your company to
do the evaluation;
you should always be evaluating
your own performance.

Michael W. Hill

"Your" Performance Evaluation

Some companies have followed the recommendations of my first book *Measuring to Manage*. These companies have employee evaluations that are based on measurable criteria; they're given twice a year and they bring out the best in employees' performance.

Whether you work for one of these companies or not you should measure your own performance.

This chapter will teach you how to put your own performance evaluation together.

A good performance evaluation starts off with a good job description. Make sure you have one. If not, make your own.

Here's what it needs to state:

- Job Title:
- Reports to:
- Overall Responsibilities:
- Tasks Performed:
- Skills and Attributes:
- Equipment Used:

What you're trying to do here is accurately capture the essence of your job. This description should allow you to know what the company expects of you. I also like to see an area in the description that states how this position fulfills some of the company's current needs and long-range objectives.

Once you have your job description it's time to move on to putting together the performance evaluation for your position.

Your first question should be: what is the major goal or objective for your position? Your second question is: how does this position support the organization's vision, mission and values? Once these two questions are answered you can start to identify specific results that, when achieved, fulfill the job description.

These results that you have identified must be measurable – based on objective statements. There is no room here for subjective statements or questions.

Please note that I used the term *results* – twice in the above paragraphs! We are looking for what results you bring to the position, not what activities you do.

Most companies make the mistake of measuring activities instead of results. Companies make money from results.

"If you can't measure it,
you can't manage it."

Peter Drucker

Management Consultant

How do we know if we've identified a result versus an activity? It's easy: apply the same SMART criteria you used to establish personal goals.

SMART is the acronym for:

S – specific
M – measurable
A – attainable
R – results-oriented
T – Time-phased

If your answers meet the above criteria you can rest assured that you will be seeing "measurable results."

EXAMPLE: Company XYZ wants its sales associates to sell to eight new accounts per month.

Specific – **M**easurable – **A**ttainable – **R**esults-oriented – Time-phased

When listing your objective criteria, avoid the words: good, many, effective, well done, successful, better, best. These words are not measurable, so they lead to subjective standards.

Let's work through the steps for your performance evaluation.

1. Identify an important result that your position needs to accomplish.
2. What goal can you attach to this accomplishment?

3. What "measurable criteria" must be present and accomplished to satisfy your goal? Be sure they are SMART.

EXAMPLE:

1. Important Result: Company XYZ wants more business from new accounts.
2. Goal: Company XYZ wants its sales associates to locate and sell eight new accounts a month.
3. Measurable Criteria: A minimum of 80 "new" accounts have been identified, (assuming a close rate of 10%). The Company goal of eight for the month will be met. A further breakdown shows that a minimum of two new accounts are needed to be "closed" per week, to equal the monthly goal.

Let me give you another:

EXAMPLE:

1. Important Result: Company XYZ wants accounts receivable to reduce the number of past due accounts.
2. Goal: Company XYZ wants its accounting associates to increase receivables from an average of 45 days outstanding to 30.

3. Measurable Criteria: A minimum of x "past due" accounts will be identified, and 25% will be called weekly.

With this type of "measurable" review your performance should easily be meeting or exceeding your company's expectations.

If your company currently has performance reviews, make sure they are based on "measurable" criteria. If they are not, get with your boss and agree on measurable criteria.

What do you do when you find yourself consistently exceeding expectations? It's probably time to ask for more responsibility!

Michael W. Hill

If your company doesn't have measurable criteria, schedule a meeting with your manager and present yours. Ask him or her to agree with the criteria. What you want to agree on is how your position with the company is going to be measured. With an evaluation form like the one you have just designed, your next question can be: if you're meeting and exceeding expectations, WIIFM? - What's in it for me?

Many companies in today's economy have frozen wages, instituted across-the-board salary reductions. What they have failed to address is what their policies have done to those employees who are exceeding expectations. If the employees' needs are not being met these individuals will look elsewhere!

Let me assure you that there are companies out there – even in today's economy- that are rewarding their high-performing employees and thus creating an atmosphere of "help us reach our (company) goals and we will help you (employee) reach your goals (raises, promotions, etc.)."

In the vast majority of companies 20 percent of the employees are doing 80 percent of the work (Pareto's Law).

There are admirable potentialities in every human being. Believe in your strength and your youth. Learn to repeat endlessly to yourself, "It all depends on me."

Andre Gide
Novelist

A quandary came up the other day with a friend of mine: Mike, I'm on the executive team and no one has ever evaluated me. My friend's situation is similar to the situation many owners find themselves in; where do you go to get reviewed?

The answer? Do it yourself! Write up your own evaluation every six months (or a shorter time frame, depending on circumstances). Write up your own evaluation based on the concepts in this chapter and fill out your own evaluation form, and hold yourself accountable! Reward yourself for a job well done or withhold a reward if you have fallen short. As long as you have made the criteria measurable you'll get a very accurate picture of how you're doing and where you need improvement.

Since the economic downturn in 2008, many companies have stopped their employee evaluations. What a mistake!

My research shows that those companies that have continued to evaluate their employees during good economies and poor ones are the companies that are outperforming their competitors. They are the ones that can more easily identify what needs to be focused on and they can direct the company assets to those issues.

Your goal after reading this book is to put yourself in that top-producing 20 percent...the group that is given the above-average raises...the group that gets the promotions... the group that is never looked at for lay-offs or cut-backs.

References

Boldt, Lawrence. 2001. *How to Be, Do, or Have Anything.*
Berkley, CA.: Ten Speed Press

Crother, Cyndi. 2004. Catch!
San Francisco: Barrett-Koehler Publishers, Inc.

DePhillps, Susan. 2005. *Corporate Confidential.*
Avon, MA.: Platinum Press

Goldsmith, Marshall. 2007. *What Got You Here Won't Get You There.*
New York: Hyperion

Mackay, Harvey. 1990. *Beware the Naked Man Who Offers You His Shirt.*
New York: William Morrow & Company Inc.

Mackay, Harvey. 1997. *Dig Your Well Before You're Thirsty.*
New York: Doubleday

Mackay, Harvey. 2005. *Fired Up.*
New York: Ballantine Books

Rath, Tom. Clifton Ph.D. Donald. 2004. *How Full Is Your Bucket.*
New York: Gallup Press

Smart, Bradford. 2005. *Topgrading.*
New York; Portfolio

Stoltz Ph.D., Paul. 2000. *Adversity Quotient at Work.*
New York:HarperCollins Publishers Inc.

Tracy, Brian. 2002. *Focal Point.*
New York: Amacon

INDEX

www.ingramcontent.com/pod-product-compliance
Lightning Source LLC
Chambersburg PA
CBHW051536170526
45165CB00002B/756

* 9 7 8 1 4 5 6 4 4 0 0 4 6 *